The Pastoral Epistles

and

Philemon

Group Study Guide

By

Paul Zeron

Small Church SOS
Bayonne, NJ

©2017 by Paul Zeron

Table of Contents

THE PASTORAL EPISTLES – GENERAL INTRODUCTION

General Introduction: The First and Second Epistles to Timothy, and the Epistle to Titus form a distinct group among the letters written by Paul, and are now known as the Pastoral Epistles because they were addressed to two Christian ministers. When Timothy and Titus received these epistles they were not acting, as they had previously done, as missionaries or itinerant evangelists, but had been left by Paul in charge of churches; the former having the oversight of the church in Ephesus, and the latter having the care of the churches in the island of Crete. The Pastoral Epistles were written to guide them in the discharge of the duties devolving upon them as Christian pastors. Such is a general description of these epistles In each of them, however, there is a great deal more than is covered or implied by the designation, "Pastoral"-- much that is personal, and much also that is concerned with Christian faith and doctrine and practice generally.

Date and order: In regard to the date of these epistles, external and internal evidence alike go to show that they belong to practically the same period. The dates of their composition are separated from each other by not more than three or four years; and the dates of each and all of them must be close to the Neronic persecution (64 AD). If Paul was executed 67 AD (Ramsay), there is only a short interval of time between his release in 61 or 62, and his death in 67, that is a period of some 5 or 6 years, during which his later travels took place, and when the Pastoral Epistles were written. "Between the three letters there is an affinity of language, a similarity of thought, and a likeness of errors combated, which prevents our referring any of them to a period much earlier than the others" (Theodore Zahn) The order in which they were written must have been 1 Timothy, Titus, 2 Timothy. It is universally acknowledged that 2 Timothy is the very last of Paul's extant epistles, and the internal evidence of the other two seems to point out 1 Timothy as earlier than Titus.

— Adapted from John Rutherford, (from International Standard Bible Encylopaedia, Electronic Database (C) 1996 by Biblesoft).

When considered in their chronological order, the Pastoral Epistles develop a narrowing focus on the ministry. 1 Timothy deals with the Ministry of Church Operations at Large, Titus with the Development of Ministers in General including the leadership of mature believers, and 2 Timothy with the Personal Development of a Minister.

1 TIMOTHY

INTRODUCTION FOR 1 TIMOTHY

Paul had left Timothy behind at Ephesus with an awesome responsibility: to charge some not to teach anything contrary to the "sound doctrine" which was according to the "glorious gospel of the blessed God" (1:3-11). Fulfilling this charge was made difficult by Timothy's youth and natural timidity (4:11-12; cf. 2Ti 1:7-8). While Paul hoped to come himself, he writes Timothy to guide him in the meantime (1Ti 3:14-15). Therefore, Paul writes:

- To instruct Timothy on how to conduct himself while administering the affairs of the church (3:14-15)
- To encourage Timothy by providing counsel concerning his own spiritual progress (4:12-16)

This letter is addressed to a young evangelist charged with the responsibility of working with a congregation and guiding them in the right way. Everything that is written is designed to aid both him and the congregation in doctrine and conduct. An appropriate theme for this epistle might therefore be: Sound doctrine for a congregation and its preacher.
— http://www.ccel.org/contrib/exec_outlines/1ti/1ti_00.htm

OUTLINE OF 1 TIMOTHY

- The Need for Strong Ministers – 1 Timothy 1:1-20
- Making a Difference – 1 Timothy 2:1-15
- The Qualification of Ministers – 1 Timothy 3:1-16
- The Character of the Ministry – 1 Timothy 4:1-16
- Ministry in the Church – 1 Timothy 5:1-6:2
- Encouragement to Ministers – 1 Timothy 6:3-21

1Tim 1:1-20   Paul, an apostle of Jesus Christ by the commandment of God our Saviour, and Lord Jesus Christ, *which is* our hope;

2Unto Timothy, *my* own son in the faith: Grace, mercy, *and* peace, from God our Father and Jesus Christ our Lord.

3As I besought thee to abide still at Ephesus, when I went into Macedonia, that thou mightest charge some that they teach no other doctrine,

4Neither give heed to fables and endless genealogies, which minister questions, rather than godly edifying which is in faith: *so do.*

5Now the end of the commandment is charity out of a pure heart, and *of* a good conscience, and *of* faith unfeigned:

6From which some having swerved have turned aside unto vain jangling;

7Desiring to be teachers of the law; understanding neither what they say, nor whereof they affirm.

8But we know that the law *is* good, if a man use it lawfully;

9Knowing this, that the law is not made for a righteous man, but for the lawless and disobedient, for the ungodly and for sinners, for unholy and profane, for murderers of fathers and murderers of mothers, for manslayers,

10For whoremongers, for them that defile themselves with mankind, for menstealers, for liars, for perjured persons, and if there be any other thing that is contrary to sound doctrine;

11According to the glorious gospel of the blessed God, which was committed to my trust.

12And I thank Christ Jesus our Lord, who hath enabled me, for that he counted me faithful, putting me into the ministry;

13Who was before a blasphemer, and a persecutor, and injurious: but I obtained mercy, because I did *it* ignorantly in unbelief.

14And the grace of our Lord was exceeding abundant with faith and love which is in Christ Jesus.

15This *is* a faithful saying, and worthy of all acceptation, that Christ Jesus came into the world to save sinners; of whom I am chief.

16Howbeit for this cause I obtained mercy, that in me first Jesus Christ might shew forth all longsuffering, for a pattern to them which should hereafter believe on him to life everlasting.

17Now unto the King eternal, immortal, invisible, the only wise God, *be* honour and glory for ever and ever. Amen.

18This charge I commit unto thee, son Timothy, according to the prophecies which went before on thee, that thou by them mightest war a good warfare;

19Holding faith, and a good conscience; which some having put away concerning faith have made shipwreck:

20Of whom is Hymenaeus and Alexander; whom I have delivered unto Satan, that they may learn not to blaspheme.

1. Look up the word hope (vs. 1) in a good Bible dictionary. What is the special meaning of this word?

_____

2. Where was Timothy to minister? (vs. 3)

_____

3. What was one of the chief problems that Timothy would have to deal with? (vs. 3)

_____

4. What would lead to doubts rather than being edified, or built up in the faith? (vs. 4)

_____

5. What three areas of Christian growth did Paul desire for the people of Ephesus? (vs. 5)

_____

6. What were the false teachers in Ephesus emphasizing? (vss. 6-7)

_____

7. Compare vss. 8, 9 to Romans 7:10, 12; 3:19, 20. In what way is the law for believers and unbelievers?

_____

_____

_____

8. Did Paul feel he deserved to be in the ministry? (vss. 12-15)

_____

9. What was supposed to be used by Timothy to strengthen him in his work? (vss. 18-19)

_____

10. Who were two chief opponents of Timothy? (vs. 20)

_____

_____

_____

_____

_____

_____

_____

_____

_____

_____

1Tim 2:1-15   I exhort therefore, that, first of all, supplications, prayers, intercessions, *and* giving of thanks, be made for all men;

2For kings, and *for* all that are in authority; that we may lead a quiet and peaceable life in all godliness and honesty.

3For this *is* good and acceptable in the sight of God our Saviour;

4Who will have all men to be saved, and to come unto the knowledge of the truth.

5For *there is* one God, and one mediator between God and men, the man Christ Jesus;

6Who gave himself a ransom for all, to be testified in due time.

7Whereunto I am ordained a preacher, and an apostle, (I speak the truth in Christ, *and* lie not;) a teacher of the Gentiles in faith and verity.

8I will therefore that men pray every where, lifting up holy hands, without wrath and doubting.

9In like manner also, that women adorn themselves in modest apparel, with shamefacedness and sobriety; not with broided hair, or gold, or pearls, or costly array;

10But (which becometh women professing godliness) with good works.

11Let the woman learn in silence with all subjection.

12But I suffer not a woman to teach, nor to usurp authority over the man, but to be in silence.

13For Adam was first formed, then Eve.

14And Adam was not deceived, but the woman being deceived was in the transgression.

15Notwithstanding she shall be saved in childbearing, if they continue in faith and charity and holiness with sobriety.

11. What four kinds of prayer are mentioned in vs. 1?

_____

_____

12. Why should we pray for kings and those in authority? (vss. 2,3)

_____

13. What is God's great desire in vss. 3, 4?

_____

14. How many mediators are there between God and men?

_____

15. How do we know that God wants people to be saved? (vs. 6)

_____

16. In our worship, how are we to pray? (vs. 8)

_____

17. In our worship, how are we to present ourselves? (vs. 9)

_____

18. Who is responsible for church leadership? (vss. 11-15)

_____

THE QUALIFICATION OF MINISTERS – 1 TIMOTHY 3:1-16

1Tim 3:1-16 This *is* a true saying, If a man desire the office of a bishop, he desireth a good work.

2A bishop then must be blameless, the husband of one wife, vigilant, sober, of good behaviour, given to hospitality, apt to teach;

3Not given to wine, no striker, not greedy of filthy lucre; but patient, not a brawler, not covetous;

4One that ruleth well his own house, having his children in subjection with all gravity;

5(For if a man know not how to rule his own house, how shall he take care of the church of God?)

6Not a novice, lest being lifted up with pride he fall into the condemnation of the devil.

7Moreover he must have a good report of them which are without; lest he fall into reproach and the snare of the devil.

8Likewise *must* the deacons *be* grave, not doubletongued, not given to much wine, not greedy of filthy lucre;

9Holding the mystery of the faith in a pure conscience.

10And let these also first be proved; then let them use the office of a deacon, being *found* blameless.

11Even so *must their* wives *be* grave, not slanderers, sober, faithful in all things.

12Let the deacons be the husbands of one wife, ruling their children and their own houses well.

13For they that have used the office of a deacon well purchase to themselves a good degree, and great boldness in the faith which is in Christ Jesus.

14These things write I unto thee, hoping to come unto thee shortly:

15But if I tarry long, that thou mayest know how thou oughtest to behave thyself in the house of God, which is the church of the living God, the pillar and ground of the truth.

16And without controversy great is the mystery of godliness: God was manifest in the flesh, justified in the Spirit, seen of angels, preached unto the Gentiles, believed on in the world, received up into glory.

19. (Answer will be given in class) What terms does the Bible use for church leadership?

a. _____

b. _____

c. _____

d. _____

20. List the qualities that a minister must have according to vss. 2-7:

_____

_____

_____

_____

21. What are the qualities of a deacon? (vss. 8-13)

_____

_____

22. Compare vss. 8-13 with Acts 6:1-4. How does the deacon's role differ from that of the pastor?

_____

_____

23. Why did Paul write these qualifications for the ministry? (vss. 14-15)

_____

24. What is the mystery of godliness? (vs. 16)

_____

BEGINNING TO FIND A NEW PASTOR

Whether a new church is just getting started or an old church loses its pastor due to illness, termination, death, or a call to a new ministry, the congregation must be prepared to call a new pastor. There are many pitfalls to be avoided in calling a new minister; many churches do what is tantamount to placing an ad in the newspaper and getting all kinds of responses that would not fit the church's personality, spiritual heritage, or doctrine. In later exercises, we will discuss further steps for calling a minister. In the space below, write down some of the qualities that a church should try to avoid in a minister. Keep in mind that what might not appear desirable by the world's standards might be qualities that the Lord requires in a man of God. Consider the following articles that were published to demonstrate this fact.

A letter to a pulpit committee—Gentlemen: Understanding your pulpit is vacant, I should like to apply for the position. I have many qualifications. I've been a preacher with much success and also some success as a writer. some say I'm a good organizer. I've been a leader most places I've been. I'm over 50 years of age. I have never preached in one place for more than three years. In some places, I have left town after my work caused riots and disturbances. I must admit I have been in jail three or four times, but not because of any real wrongdoing. My health is not too good, though I still get a great deal done. The churches I have preached in have been small, though located in several large cities. I've not gotten along well with religious leaders in towns where I have preached. In fact, some have threatened me and even attacked me physically. I am not too good at keeping records. I have been know to forget whom I have baptized. However, if you can use me, I shall do my best for you. Sincerely, Paul.

The Perfect Pastor—Results of a computerized survey indicate that the perfect pastor preaches exactly 15 minutes. He condemns sin, but never embarrasses anyone. He works from 8 a.m. until midnight and is also the janitor. He makes $60 a week, wears good clothes, drives a new car, and gives $50 a week to the poor. He is 28 years old, has been preaching for 25 years, is wonderfully gentle and handsome, loves to work with teenagers and spends countless hours with senior citizens. He makes 15 calls daily on parish families, shut-ins and hospital patients, and is always in his office when needed. If your pastor does not measure up, simply send this letter to six other parishes that are tired of their pastors, too. Then bundle up your pastor and send him to the church at the top of the list. In one week you will receive 1,643 pastors. One of them should be perfect.

PREPARING TO CALL A PASTOR

Make a list of doctrines that a church should make sure a prospective pastor believes.

_____

_____

_____

_____

_____

_____

_____

_____

_____

_____

_____

_____

_____

_____

_____

_____

_____

_____

_____

_____

_____

_____

_____

_____

_____

_____

_____

_____

_____

_____

SPECIAL ASSIGNMENT

Use the following survey to find out how other denominations qualify and select ministers. Call ministers from various denominations and tell them your name and that you are from Peoples Baptist Church; you are calling as part of a special assignment in the adult Bible class to find out more about how other churches get a pastor. Ask if they would be able to take a few minutes to answer four questions or if there would be another time you might call when it is more convenient for them. Record their responses below. Use extra paper, if needed.

1. What educational or other requirements would your church have for a pastor?
2. What steps does a person have to take to become a minister in your denomination?
3. What is the process for a minister to become a pastor of a church in your denomination?
4. In what ways might a minister be called to leave a church in your denomination?

_____

_____

_____

_____

_____

_____

1Tim 4:1-16 Now the Spirit speaketh expressly, that in the latter times some shall depart from the faith, giving heed to seducing spirits, and doctrines of devils;
2Speaking lies in hypocrisy; having their conscience seared with a hot iron;
3Forbidding to marry, *and commanding* to abstain from meats, which God hath created to be received with thanksgiving of them which believe and know the truth.
4For every creature of God *is* good, and nothing to be refused, if it be received with thanksgiving:
5For it is sanctified by the word of God and prayer.
6If thou put the brethren in remembrance of these things, thou shalt be a good minister of Jesus Christ, nourished up in the words of faith and of good doctrine, whereunto thou hast attained.
7But refuse profane and old wives' fables, and exercise thyself *rather* unto godliness.
8For bodily exercise profiteth little: but godliness is profitable unto all things, having promise of the life that now is, and of that which is to come.
9This *is* a faithful saying and worthy of all acceptation.
10For therefore we both labour and suffer reproach, because we trust in the living God, who is the Saviour of all men, specially of those that believe.
11These things command and teach.
12Let no man despise thy youth; but be thou an example of the believers, in word, in conversation, in charity, in spirit, in faith, in purity.
13Till I come, give attendance to reading, to exhortation, to doctrine.
14Neglect not the gift that is in thee, which was given thee by prophecy, with the laying on of the hands of the presbytery.
15Meditate upon these things; give thyself wholly to them; that thy profiting may appear to all.
16Take heed unto thyself, and unto the doctrine; continue in them: for in doing this thou shalt both save thyself, and them that hear thee.

25. List the "doctrines of devils" in vss. 1-5:

26. What are we to avoid and what are we to seek after according to vss. 6-9?

27. Who will be saved? (vs. 10)

28. What things should a minister be sure to develop in his ministry? (vss. 11-16)

1Tim 5:1-25 Rebuke not an elder, but intreat *him* as a father; *and* the younger men as brethren;

2The elder women as mothers; the younger as sisters, with all purity.

3Honour widows that are widows indeed.

4But if any widow have children or nephews, let them learn first to shew piety at home, and to requite their parents: for that is good and acceptable before God.

5Now she that is a widow indeed, and desolate, trusteth in God, and continueth in supplications and prayers night and day.

6But she that liveth in pleasure is dead while she liveth.

7And these things give in charge, that they may be blameless.

8But if any provide not for his own, and specially for those of his own house, he hath denied the faith, and is worse than an infidel.

9Let not a widow be taken into the number under threescore years old, having been the wife of one man,

10Well reported of for good works; if she have brought up children, if she have lodged strangers, if she have washed the saints' feet, if she have relieved the afflicted, if she have diligently followed every good work.

11But the younger widows refuse: for when they have begun to wax wanton against Christ, they will marry;

12Having damnation, because they have cast off their first faith.

13And withal they learn *to be* idle, wandering about from house to house; and not only idle, but tattlers also and busybodies, speaking things which they ought not.

14I will therefore that the younger women marry, bear children, guide the house, give none occasion to the adversary to speak reproachfully.

15For some are already turned aside after Satan.

16If any man or woman that believeth have widows, let them relieve them, and let not the church be charged; that it may relieve them that are widows indeed.

17Let the elders that rule well be counted worthy of double honour, especially they who labour in the word and doctrine.

18For the scripture saith, Thou shalt not muzzle the ox that treadeth out the corn. And, The labourer *is* worthy of his reward.

19Against an elder receive not an accusation, but before two or three witnesses.

20Them that sin rebuke before all, that others also may fear.

21I charge *thee* before God, and the Lord Jesus Christ, and the elect angels, that thou observe these things without preferring one before another, doing nothing by partiality.

22Lay hands suddenly on no man, neither be partaker of other men's sins: keep thyself pure.

23Drink no longer water, but use a little wine for thy stomach's sake and thine often infirmities.

24Some men's sins are open beforehand, going before to judgment; and some *men* they follow after.

25Likewise also the good works *of some* are manifest beforehand; and they that are otherwise cannot be hid.

1Tim 6:1-21 Let as many servants as are under the yoke count their own masters worthy of all honour, that the name of God and *his* doctrine be not blasphemed.

2And they that have believing masters, let them not despise *them*, because they are brethren; but rather do *them* service, because they are faithful and beloved, partakers of the benefit. These things teach and exhort.

29. How are we to treat men in the church? (vs. 1)

_____

30. How are we to treat women in the church? (vss. 2, 3)

_____

31. What two kinds of widows are there? (vss. 3-7)

_____

32. How are widows to be treated? (vss. 8-16)

_____

_____

33. How are the church elders to be taken care of? (vss. 17-18)

_____

34. If there is a problem with an elder, what two ways should it be handled? (vss. 19-20)

_____

_____

35. What should we be careful not to do in dealing with leaders in the church? (vs. 21)

_____

36. What two things should we avoid in dealing with the problems of others? (vs. 22)

_____

37. What kind of wine is referred to in vs. 23?

_____

38. What should our attitude in general be about the final judgment of anyone? (vss. 24, 25)

_____

_____

39. How should employers and employees treat each other? (6:1, 2)

_____

_____

1 Tim 6:3-21 If any man teach otherwise, and consent not to wholesome words, *even* the words of our Lord Jesus Christ, and to the doctrine which is according to godliness;

4He is proud, knowing nothing, but doting about questions and strifes of words, whereof cometh envy, strife, railings, evil surmisings,

5Perverse disputings of men of corrupt minds, and destitute of the truth, supposing that gain is godliness: from such withdraw thyself.

6But godliness with contentment is great gain.

7For we brought nothing into *this* world, *and it is* certain we can carry nothing out.

8And having food and raiment let us be therewith content.

9But they that will be rich fall into temptation and a snare, and *into* many foolish and hurtful lusts, which drown men in destruction and perdition.

10For the love of money is the root of all evil: which while some coveted after, they have erred from the faith, and pierced themselves through with many sorrows.

11But thou, O man of God, flee these things; and follow after righteousness, godliness, faith, love, patience, meekness.

12Fight the good fight of faith, lay hold on eternal life, whereunto thou art also called, and hast professed a good profession before many witnesses.

13I give thee charge in the sight of God, who quickeneth all things, and *before* Christ Jesus, who before Pontius Pilate witnessed a good confession;

14That thou keep *this* commandment without spot, unrebukeable, until the appearing of our Lord Jesus Christ:

15Which in his times he shall shew, *who is* the blessed and only Potentate, the King of kings, and Lord of lords;

16Who only hath immortality, dwelling in the light which no man can approach unto; whom no man hath seen, nor can see: to whom *be* honour and power everlasting. Amen.

17Charge them that are rich in this world, that they be not highminded, nor trust in uncertain riches, but in the living God, who giveth us richly all things to enjoy;

18That they do good, that they be rich in good works, ready to distribute, willing to communicate;

19Laying up in store for themselves a good foundation against the time to come, that they may lay hold on eternal life.

20O Timothy, keep that which is committed to thy trust, avoiding profane *and* vain babblings, and oppositions of science falsely so called:

21Which some professing have erred concerning the faith. Grace *be* with thee. Amen.

40. How can a person be described who does not follow the teachings of the Bible? (vss. 3-5)

_____

_____

_____

41. What is "great gain"? (vss. 6-8)

_____

42. What will trap many people? (vss. 9-10)

_____

43. What should we be pursuing according to vss. 11 and 12?

_____

_____

44. What should those that are rich do? (vss. 17-19)

_____

_____

45. What should those who minister avoid? (vss. 20-21)

_____

_____

2 TIMOTHY

INTRODUCTION FOR 2 TIMOTHY

The first letter to Timothy and the one to Titus were written during travel and missionary work between Paul's two Roman imprisonments. A date somewhere between A. D. 61 and 63 can be set, because the Second Epistle to Timothy contains Paul's farewell address (2 Tim. 4:6-8), the last words from the apostle shortly before his martyrdom, generally set between A. D. 65 and 68.

First and Second Timothy differ in historical context. In the first epistle Paul writes from Macedonia to young Timothy (1 Tim. 4:12), who has been left in Ephesus to oversee the congregation (1 Tim. 1:3). The second epistle, also written to Timothy in Ephesus (2 Tim. 1:18), comes from Rome where Paul is undergoing a second (2 Tim. 4:16) and harsher imprisonment (2 Tim. 1:18, 16; 2:9). Paul is alone (except for Luke, 2 Tim. 4:11), and he knows the end of his life will come soon (2 Tim. 4:6). One can almost hear the plaintive echo of the apostle's voice as he bids Timothy to "come quickly before winter" (2 Tim. 4:9,21).

The occasion for both epistles is much the same. Paul is deeply troubled by false teaching (1 Tim. 1:3-11; 2 Tim. 2:23) and apostasy (1 Tim. 1:6; 4:1; 2 Tim. 3:1-9) which endanger the church at Ephesus. He warns Timothy to beware of fables and endless genealogies (1 Tim. 1:4; 4:7; 2 Tim. 4:4), idle gossip (1 Tim. 5:13; 2 Tim. 2:16), rigid lifestyles based on the denial of things (1 Tim. 4:3), the snares of wealth (1 Tim. 6:9-10,17-19), and religious speculations (1 Tim. 6:20). He warns that apostasy, in whatever form, will spread like cancer (2 Tim. 2:17). Paul urges Timothy to combat its malignant growth by teaching sound doctrine, promoting good works, and accepting one's share of suffering for the sake of the gospel (2 Tim. 1:8; 2:3, 11-13).

The message of 1 and 2 Timothy can be summed up by words like remember (2 Tim. 2:8), guard (1 Tim. 6:20), be strong (2 Tim. 2:1), and commit (1 Tim. 1:18; 2:2). For Paul, the best medicine for false teaching and apostasy is "sound doctrine" (1 Tim. 1:10; 4:3). The Epistles to Timothy might be considered our earliest manual of church organization. Within them we find guidelines for the selection of church leaders (1 Tim. 3:1-13).

— (from Nelson's Illustrated Bible Dictionary, Copyright (C) 1986, Thomas Nelson Publishers)

1 Timothy focused on the operation of the church and had some personal remarks for Timothy. Now, 2 Timothy focuses on the personal with a minor emphasis on the operation of the church. This might be especially so because the apostle Paul was about to die and would have emphasized those things that a father might say to a son as his last remarks. The book of 2 Timothy is about the character of a minister of Christ and so we should apply this portion of God's Word in a very personal way to our lives and service to Him.

18

OUTLINE OF 2 TIMOTHY

- Thankfulness for the soldier of Christ. 1:1-7
- The Call of a soldier of Christ. 1:8-18
- The Character of a soldier of Christ. 2:1-26
- The Caution for a soldier of Christ. 3:1-17
- The Charge to a Soldier of Christ. 4:1-5
- The Comfort of a soldier of Christ. 4:6-18

— (Adapted from the Ryrie Study Bible, ©1978, Moody Press)

THANKFULNESS FOR THE SOLDIER OF CHRIST – 2 TIMOTHY 1:1-7

2Tim 1:1-7 Paul, an apostle of Jesus Christ by the will of God, according to the promise of life which is in Christ Jesus,

2To Timothy, *my* dearly beloved son: Grace, mercy, *and* peace, from God the Father and Christ Jesus our Lord.

3I thank God, whom I serve from *my* forefathers with pure conscience, that without ceasing I have remembrance of thee in my prayers night and day;

4Greatly desiring to see thee, being mindful of thy tears, that I may be filled with joy;

5When I call to remembrance the unfeigned faith that is in thee, which dwelt first in thy grandmother Lois, and thy mother Eunice; and I am persuaded that in thee also.

6Wherefore I put thee in remembrance that thou stir up the gift of God, which is in thee by the putting on of my hands.

7For God hath not given us the spirit of fear; but of power, and of love, and of a sound mind.

46. How did Paul choose to remember Timothy? (vs. 3)

_____

47. What kind of faith did Paul admire in Timothy? (vs.5)

_____

48. Who passed on their faith to Timothy? (vs. 5)

_____

49. What three things did God bestow on us as soldiers of Christ? (vs. 7)

_____

_____

_____

2Tim 1:8-18 Be not thou therefore ashamed of the testimony of our Lord, nor of me his prisoner: but be thou partaker of the afflictions of the gospel according to the power of God;

9Who hath saved us, and called *us* with an holy calling, not according to our works, but according to his own purpose and grace, which was given us in Christ Jesus before the world began,

10But is now made manifest by the appearing of our Saviour Jesus Christ, who hath abolished death, and hath brought life and immortality to light through the gospel:

11Whereunto I am appointed a preacher, and an apostle, and a teacher of the Gentiles.

12For the which cause I also suffer these things: nevertheless I am not ashamed: for I know whom I have believed, and am persuaded that he is able to keep that which I have committed unto him against that day.

13Hold fast the form of sound words, which thou hast heard of me, in faith and love which is in Christ Jesus.

14That good thing which was committed unto thee keep by the Holy Ghost which dwelleth in us.

15This thou knowest, that all they which are in Asia be turned away from me; of whom are Phygellus and Hermogenes.

16The Lord give mercy unto the house of Onesiphorus; for he oft refreshed me, and was not ashamed of my chain:

17But, when he was in Rome, he sought me out very diligently, and found *me*.

18The Lord grant unto him that he may find mercy of the Lord in that day: and in how many things he ministered unto me at Ephesus, thou knowest very well.

50.   What three things did Paul not want Timothy to be ashamed of? (vs. 8)

_____

_____

_____

51. Why should we not be ashamed? (vss. 9-12)

_____

_____

52. What should we hold fast to? (vs. 13)

_____

THE CHARACTER OF A SOLDIER OF CHRIST – 2 TIMOTHY 2:1-26

2Tim 2:1-26 Thou therefore, my son, be strong in the grace that is in Christ Jesus.

2And the things that thou hast heard of me among many witnesses, the same commit thou to faithful men, who shall be able to teach others also.

3Thou therefore endure hardness, as a good soldier of Jesus Christ.

4No man that warreth entangleth himself with the affairs of *this* life; that he may please him who hath chosen him to be a soldier.

5And if a man also strive for masteries, *yet* is he not crowned, except he strive lawfully.

6The husbandman that laboureth must be first partaker of the fruits.

7Consider what I say; and the Lord give thee understanding in all things.

8Remember that Jesus Christ of the seed of David was raised from the dead according to my gospel:

9Wherein I suffer trouble, as an evil doer, *even* unto bonds; but the word of God is not bound.

10Therefore I endure all things for the elect's sakes, that they may also obtain the salvation which is in Christ Jesus with eternal glory.

11 *It is* a faithful saying: For if we be dead with *him*, we shall also live with *him*:

12If we suffer, we shall also reign with *him*: if we deny *him*, he also will deny us:

13If we believe not, *yet* he abideth faithful: he cannot deny himself.

14Of these things put *them* in remembrance, charging *them* before the Lord that they strive not about words to no profit, *but* to the subverting of the hearers.

15Study to shew thyself approved unto God, a workman that needeth not to be ashamed, rightly dividing the word of truth.

16But shun profane *and* vain babblings: for they will increase unto more ungodliness.

17And their word will eat as doth a canker: of whom is Hymenaeus and Philetus;

18Who concerning the truth have erred, saying that the resurrection is past already; and overthrow the faith of some.

19Nevertheless the foundation of God standeth sure, having this seal, The Lord knoweth them that are his. And, Let every one that nameth the name of Christ depart from iniquity.

20But in a great house there are not only vessels of gold and of silver, but also of wood and of earth; and some to honour, and some to dishonour.

21If a man therefore purge himself from these, he shall be a vessel unto honour, sanctified, and meet for the master's use, *and* prepared unto every good work.

22Flee also youthful lusts: but follow righteousness, faith, charity, peace, with them that call on the Lord out of a pure heart.

23But foolish and unlearned questions avoid, knowing that they do gender strifes.

24And the servant of the Lord must not strive; but be gentle unto all *men*, apt to teach, patient,

25In meekness instructing those that oppose themselves; if God peradventure will give them repentance to the acknowledging of the truth;

26And *that* they may recover themselves out of the snare of the devil, who are taken captive by him at his will.

53. What does Paul call for Timothy to do in verses 1 and 3?

_____

54. What was Timothy to do with the spiritual things that he received? (vs. 2)

_____

55. What two things should a soldier of Christ avoid? (vss. 4, 5)

_____

_____

56. What should the soldier of Christ not avoid according to verse 6?

_____

57. What motivation does Paul give for being a soldier of Christ? (vss. 7-13)

_____

_____

58. What did Paul want Timothy to remind people of in verse 14?

_____

59. What should the soldier of Christ be sure to do according to verse 15?

_____

60. What will profane and vain babblings do for the soldier of Christ? (vss. 16, 17)

_____

61. How will a soldier of Christ be a vessel of honor? (vss. 18-21)

_____

62. What should the soldier of Christ do to purge himself? (vss. 22-23)

_____

63. What should be the general approach of the soldier of Christ be? (vs. 24)

_____

64. Who will be the one to convince people of the truth? (vs. 25)

_____

65. What will be the result of one submitting themselves to God? (vs. 26)

_____

2Tim 3:1-17 This know also, that in the last days perilous times shall come.

2For men shall be lovers of their own selves, covetous, boasters, proud, blasphemers, disobedient to parents, unthankful, unholy,

3Without natural affection, trucebreakers, false accusers, incontinent, fierce, despisers of those that are good,

4Traitors, heady, highminded, lovers of pleasures more than lovers of God;

5Having a form of godliness, but denying the power thereof: from such turn away.

6For of this sort are they which creep into houses, and lead captive silly women laden with sins, led away with divers lusts,

7Ever learning, and never able to come to the knowledge of the truth.

8Now as Jannes and Jambres withstood Moses, so do these also resist the truth: men of corrupt minds, reprobate concerning the faith.

9But they shall proceed no further: for their folly shall be manifest unto all *men*, as theirs also was.

10But thou hast fully known my doctrine, manner of life, purpose, faith, longsuffering, charity, patience,

11Persecutions, afflictions, which came unto me at Antioch, at Iconium, at Lystra; what persecutions I endured: but out of *them* all the Lord delivered me.

12Yea, and all that will live godly in Christ Jesus shall suffer persecution.

13But evil men and seducers shall wax worse and worse, deceiving, and being deceived.

14But continue thou in the things which thou hast learned and hast been assured of, knowing of whom thou hast learned *them*;

15And that from a child thou hast known the holy scriptures, which are able to make thee wise unto salvation through faith which is in Christ Jesus.

16All scripture *is* given by inspiration of God, and *is* profitable for doctrine, for reproof, for correction, for instruction in righteousness:

17That the man of God may be perfect, throughly furnished unto all good works.

66. What shall come in the last days? (vs. 1)

_____

67. What will be the condition of mankind in the last days? (vss. 2-4)

_____

_____

_____

68. What will the leaders of this world be like? (vss. 8)

_____

69. Will they be hard to identify? (vs. 9)

_____

70. What does Paul refer to show that he is a true soldier of Christ? (vss. 10-11)

_____

71. What can the soldier of Christ expect to happen to him which will show that he is a true soldier? (vs. 12)

_____

72. Will the spiritual condition of this world improve as a result of our labors? (vs. 13)

_____

73. Inspite of the world's spiritual conditon, what should we persist in? (vss. 14-15)

_____

74. How was Scripture given to us? (vs.16)

_____

75. What can the Scriptures be used for? (vss. 16)

_____

_____

76. What will be the result of the use of the Scripture? (vs. 17)

_____

The Charge to a Soldier of Christ – 2 Timothy 4:1-5

2Tim 4:1-5 I charge *thee* therefore before God, and the Lord Jesus Christ, who shall judge the quick and the dead at his appearing and his kingdom;

2Preach the word; be instant in season, out of season; reprove, rebuke, exhort with all longsuffering and doctrine.

3For the time will come when they will not endure sound doctrine; but after their own lusts shall they heap to themselves teachers, having itching ears;

4And they shall turn away *their* ears from the truth, and shall be turned unto fables.

5But watch thou in all things, endure afflictions, do the work of an evangelist, make full proof of thy ministry.

77. Who does Paul call as a witness of the charge he gives to Timothy? (vs. 1)

_____

78. What is the primary charge he gives to Timothy? (vs. 2)

_____

79. Under what conditions is Timothy to carry out his charge? (vs. 2)

_____

80. What four things is Timothy to do as he carries out his charge? (vs. 2)

_____

_____

_____

81. What three things will happen after people get tired of hearing the Word preached to them? (vss. 3,4)

_____

_____

_____

82. What three things accompanies making "full proof" of the ministry? (vs. 5)

_____

_____

_____

2Tim 4:6-22 For I am now ready to be offered, and the time of my departure is at hand.

7I have fought a good fight, I have finished *my* course, I have kept the faith:

8Henceforth there is laid up for me a crown of righteousness, which the Lord, the righteous judge, shall give me at that day: and not to me only, but unto all them also that love his appearing.

9Do thy diligence to come shortly unto me:

10For Demas hath forsaken me, having loved this present world, and is departed unto Thessalonica; Crescens to Galatia, Titus unto Dalmatia.

11Only Luke is with me. Take Mark, and bring him with thee: for he is profitable to me for the ministry.

12And Tychicus have I sent to Ephesus.

13The cloke that I left at Troas with Carpus, when thou comest, bring *with thee*, and the books, *but* especially the parchments.

14Alexander the coppersmith did me much evil: the Lord reward him according to his works:

15Of whom be thou ware also; for he hath greatly withstood our words.

16At my first answer no man stood with me, but all *men* forsook me: *I pray God* that it may not be laid to their charge.

17Notwithstanding the Lord stood with me, and strengthened me; that by me the preaching might be fully known, and *that* all the Gentiles might hear: and I was delivered out of the mouth of the lion.

18And the Lord shall deliver me from every evil work, and will preserve *me* unto his heavenly kingdom: to whom *be* glory for ever and ever. Amen.

19Salute Prisca and Aquila, and the household of Onesiphorus.

20Erastus abode at Corinth: but Trophimus have I left at Miletum sick.

21Do thy diligence to come before winter. Eubulus greeteth thee, and Pudens, and Linus, and Claudia, and all the brethren.

22The Lord Jesus Christ *be* with thy spirit. Grace *be* with you. Amen.

83. What was Paul ready for? (vs. 6)

_____

84. What three things made Paul ready? (vs. 7)

_____

_____

_____

85. What was Paul looking forward to receiving? (vs. 8)

_____

86. What was the difference between Demas and Mark? (vss. 10, 11)

_____

_____

87. What did Paul want Timothy to bring with him? (vs. 13)

_____

88. What two things was Timothy to do about Alexander the coppersmith? (vss. 14, 15)

_____

_____

89. What was Paul trusting the Lord for? (vss. 16-18)

_____

_____

90. How does Paul close his letter to Timothy? (vs. 22)

_____

TITUS

INTRODUCTION FOR TITUS

This epistle was written before 2 Timothy, which is the last of Paul's extant writings. Titus was a Gentile and Paul's disciple. In the Second Epistle to the Corinthians, he is mentioned nine times and two times in the Epistle to the Galatians. It was Titus who brought to Paul the manner in which the Corintians received his First Epistle, and it was Titus who carried back to that church the Second Epistle.

It seems evident from Titus 1:5 that Paul visited the church on the island of Crete, which lies in the Greek Archipelago, and left Titus in charge of the work. That was when Paul returned to Asia from his first imprisonment in Rome. There were many Jews on the island, some of whom were probably at Jerusalem on the Day of Pentecost (Acts 2:11), and it is thought by some that these converts to Christianity returned to Crete and founded there a Christian comunity. This epistle was written from Nicopolis probably shortly before Paul was taken the second time a prisoner to Rome (67 or 68 A.D.). From 2 Timothy 4:10 we learn that Titus had been with Paul during this imprisonment.

— Adapted from The New Analytical Bible and Dictionary of the Bible, (C) 1973 by the John A. Dickson Publishing Co.

The Epistle to Titus is most related to the 1 Timothy in that it deals with the larger concern of ministers in the church; 2 Timothy is more concerned with ministry on a personal level. However, Titus is more narrowly focused in that it does not really deal with church order. Some of the elements in Titus will be closely related to 1 Timothy.

OUTLINE OF TITUS

- The need for mature leadership. 1:1-16
- The character of mature believers in leadership. 2:1-15
- General charge for mature believers. 3:1-15

Titus 1:1-16 Paul, a servant of God, and an apostle of Jesus Christ, according to the faith of God's elect, and the acknowledging of the truth which is after godliness;

2In hope of eternal life, which God, that cannot lie, promised before the world began;

3But hath in due times manifested his word through preaching, which is committed unto me according to the commandment of God our Saviour;

4To Titus, *mine* own son after the common faith: Grace, mercy, *and* peace, from God the Father and the Lord Jesus Christ our Saviour.

5For this cause left I thee in Crete, that thou shouldest set in order the things that are wanting, and ordain elders in every city, as I had appointed thee:

6If any be blameless, the husband of one wife, having faithful children not accused of riot or unruly.

7For a bishop must be blameless, as the steward of God; not selfwilled, not soon angry, not given to wine, no striker, not given to filthy lucre;

8But a lover of hospitality, a lover of good men, sober, just, holy, temperate;

9Holding fast the faithful word as he hath been taught, that he may be able by sound doctrine both to exhort and to convince the gainsayers.

10For there are many unruly and vain talkers and deceivers, specially they of the circumcision:

11Whose mouths must be stopped, who subvert whole houses, teaching things which they ought not, for filthy lucre's sake.

12One of themselves, *even* a prophet of their own, said, The Cretians *are* alway liars, evil beasts, slow bellies.

13This witness is true. Wherefore rebuke them sharply, that they may be sound in the faith;

14Not giving heed to Jewish fables, and commandments of men, that turn from the truth.

15Unto the pure all things *are* pure: but unto them that are defiled and unbelieving *is* nothing pure; but even their mind and conscience is defiled.

16They profess that they know God; but in works they deny *him*, being abominable, and disobedient, and unto every good work reprobate.

91. When did God provide for eternal life? (vs. 2)

_____

92. How does God get his message out about salvation? (vs.3)

_____

93. Why did Paul leave Titus in Crete? (vs. 5)

_____

94. List the qualifications of an elder according to vss. 6-8:

_____

_____

_____

95. What should a minister especially be careful of in his ministry? (vss. 9-11)

_____

96. How are the ungodly described in vs. 12?

_____

97. How should a minister deal with spiritual slothfulness? (vss. 13, 14)

_____

98. How are the pure and the defiled characterized in vss. 15, 16?

_____

_____

Titus 2:1-15 But speak thou the things which become sound doctrine:

2That the aged men be sober, grave, temperate, sound in faith, in charity, in patience.

3The aged women likewise, that *they be* in behaviour as becometh holiness, not false accusers, not given to much wine, teachers of good things;

4That they may teach the young women to be sober, to love their husbands, to love their children,

5 *To be* discreet, chaste, keepers at home, good, obedient to their own husbands, that the word of God be not blasphemed.

6Young men likewise exhort to be sober minded.

7In all things shewing thyself a pattern of good works: in doctrine *shewing* uncorruptness, gravity, sincerity,

8Sound speech, that cannot be condemned; that he that is of the contrary part may be ashamed, having no evil thing to say of you.

9 *Exhort* servants to be obedient unto their own masters, *and* to please *them* well in all *things*; not answering again;

10Not purloining, but shewing all good fidelity; that they may adorn the doctrine of God our Saviour in all things.

11For the grace of God that bringeth salvation hath appeared to all men,

12Teaching us that, denying ungodliness and worldly lusts, we should live soberly, righteously, and godly, in this present world;

13Looking for that blessed hope, and the glorious appearing of the great God and our Saviour Jesus Christ;

14Who gave himself for us, that he might redeem us from all iniquity, and purify unto himself a peculiar people, zealous of good works.

15These things speak, and exhort, and rebuke with all authority. Let no man despise thee.

99. In a minister's communication, he should be careful to do what?

_____

100. What should be part of the character of older, spiritual men? (vs. 2)

_____

_____

101. What should be part of the character of older, spiritual women? (vs. 3)

_____

102. What should the older women teach the younger women? (vss. 4, 5)

_____

_____

103. What should the young men especially learn according to vs. 8?

_____

_____

104. What things should employees strive for in their spiritual lives? (vss. 9, 10)

_____

_____

105. According to vss. 11–14, what should motivate us to strive for spiritual development?

_____

106. How should a minister conduct himself according to vs. 15?

_____

General Charge for Mature Believers – Titus 3:1-15

Titus 3:1-15 Put them in mind to be subject to principalities and powers, to obey magistrates, to be ready to every good work,

2To speak evil of no man, to be no brawlers, *but* gentle, shewing all meekness unto all men.

3For we ourselves also were sometimes foolish, disobedient, deceived, serving divers lusts and pleasures, living in malice and envy, hateful, *and* hating one another.

4But after that the kindness and love of God our Saviour toward man appeared,

5Not by works of righteousness which we have done, but according to his mercy he saved us, by the washing of regeneration, and renewing of the Holy Ghost;

6Which he shed on us abundantly through Jesus Christ our Saviour;

7That being justified by his grace, we should be made heirs according to the hope of eternal life.

8 *This is* a faithful saying, and these things I will that thou affirm constantly, that they which have believed in God might be careful to maintain good works. These things are good and profitable unto men.

9But avoid foolish questions, and genealogies, and contentions, and strivings about the law; for they are unprofitable and vain.

10A man that is an heretick after the first and second admonition reject;

11Knowing that he that is such is subverted, and sinneth, being condemned of himself.

12When I shall send Artemas unto thee, or Tychicus, be diligent to come unto me to Nicopolis: for I have determined there to winter.

13Bring Zenas the lawyer and Apollos on their journey diligently, that nothing be wanting unto them.

14And let ours also learn to maintain good works for necessary uses, that they be not unfruitful.

15All that are with me salute thee. Greet them that love us in the faith. Grace *be* with you all. Amen.

107. What should our attitude be to the government? (vs. 1)

_____

108. Why should we be understanding and patient with all men? (vss. 2-5)

_____

109. Why should we do good works according to verses 8-14?

_____

110. At what point should we ultimately reject a heretic? (vss. 9-11)

_____

PHILEMON

INTRODUCTION

This is a private letter, the only one of the kind written by Paul, and the shortest of his epistles. Philemon was a resident of Colossae and was a member of the church there (Col. 4:9). It was by the apostle he was brought into the Christian life...That Philemon was an earnest Christian appears from Paul's statements.

Onesimus was the slave of Philemon. In some way he had wronged his master. He came to Rome and was brought into contact with Paul. These relations resulted in his conversion. He was very serviceable to Paul who would have been glad to retain him, but he convinced him it was his duty to return to his master.

In this letter he bespeaks for Onesimus a kind and Christian resecption. It is a masterpiece of Christian courtesy and intercession. It is quite probable that the apostle was called upon many times to render such services in behalf of others.

This is one of the four "Prison Epistles," the others being Ephesians, Philippians and Colossians. It was written at Rome during the first imprisonment (62-63 A.D.).
– The New Analytical Bible, John Dickson Publisher

OUTLINE OF PHILEMON

Greetings (1–3)
Thanksgiving and Prayer (4–7)
Paul's Plea for Onesimus (8–21)
Final Request, Greetings and Benediction (22–25)

Phlm 1:1-25 Paul, a prisoner of Jesus Christ, and Timothy *our* brother, unto Philemon our dearly beloved, and fellowlabourer,

2And to *our* beloved Apphia, and Archippus our fellowsoldier, and to the church in thy house:

3Grace to you, and peace, from God our Father and the Lord Jesus Christ.

4I thank my God, making mention of thee always in my prayers,

5Hearing of thy love and faith, which thou hast toward the Lord Jesus, and toward all saints;

6That the communication of thy faith may become effectual by the acknowledging of every good thing which is in you in Christ Jesus.

7For we have great joy and consolation in thy love, because the bowels of the saints are refreshed by thee, brother.

8Wherefore, though I might be much bold in Christ to enjoin thee that which is convenient,

9Yet for love's sake I rather beseech *thee*, being such an one as Paul the aged, and now also a prisoner of Jesus Christ.

10I beseech thee for my son Onesimus, whom I have begotten in my bonds:

11Which in time past was to thee unprofitable, but now profitable to thee and to me:

12Whom I have sent again: thou therefore receive him, that is, mine own bowels:

13Whom I would have retained with me, that in thy stead he might have ministered unto me in the bonds of the gospel:

14But without thy mind would I do nothing; that thy benefit should not be as it were of necessity, but willingly.

15For perhaps he therefore departed for a season, that thou shouldest receive him for ever;

16Not now as a servant, but above a servant, a brother beloved, specially to me, but how much more unto thee, both in the flesh, and in the Lord?

17If thou count me therefore a partner, receive him as myself.

18If he hath wronged thee, or oweth *thee* ought, put that on mine account;

19I Paul have written *it* with mine own hand, I will repay *it*: albeit I do not say to thee how thou owest unto me even thine own self besides.

20Yea, brother, let me have joy of thee in the Lord: refresh my bowels in the Lord.

21Having confidence in thy obedience I wrote unto thee, knowing that thou wilt also do more than I say.

22But withal prepare me also a lodging: for I trust that through your prayers I shall be given unto you.

23There salute thee Epaphras, my fellowprisoner in Christ Jesus;

24Marcus, Aristarchus, Demas, Lucas, my fellowlabourers.

25The grace of our Lord Jesus Christ *be* with your spirit. Amen.

111.   What indicates that Philemon was a Godly man in vs. 2?

_____

112.   What did Philemon have a reputation for? (vs. 5-7)

_____

_____

113.   What made Onesimus special to Paul? (vs. 9-10)

_____

114.   What reputation did Onesimus have according to vs. 11?

_____

_____

115.   Why did Paul not assume that he could just keep Onesimus with him? (vs. 14)

_____

_____

116.   What consolation did Paul offer Philemon? (vs. 15,16)

_____

_____

117.   What relationship did Paul depend on to encourage Philemon? (vs. 17)

_____

118.   What did Paul offer to do to be perfectly fair to Philemon? (vs. 18,19)

_____

119.   Why should Philemon not necessarily require payment from Paul? (vs. 19)

_____

120.   What did Paul hope to do according to vs. 22?

_____

121.   How do Philemon, Paul, and Onesimus typify the Father, the Son, and the sinner?

_____

_____

_____

_____

_____

_____

_____

_____

SPECIAL NOTES ON SLAVERY

The first distinction is that people sold themselves (not others) into servitude. In the Old Testament, the type of "slavery" sanctioned is not forcible. It is something a person voluntarily enters into in exchange for money or a service. This is amply proven by the following passages in the books of Exodus and Deuteronomy:

Exod 21:16 And he that stealeth a man, and selleth him, or if he be found in his hand, he shall surely be put to death.

Deut 23:15-16 Thou shalt not deliver unto his master the servant which is escaped from his master unto thee:
16He shall dwell with thee, *even* among you, in that place which he shall choose in one of thy gates, where it liketh him best: thou shalt not oppress him.

An exception to this is in cases of criminal conduct. A person caught stealing was required to make restitution to the victim, and if he could not, he was sold and the money given to the victim, as detailed in Exodus

> Exod 22:3 If the sun be risen upon him, *there shall be* blood *shed* for him; *for* he should make full restitution; if he have nothing, then he shall be sold for his theft.

This certainly has similarities with our modern penal codes, in which criminals are sometimes sentenced to "imprisonment with hard labor."

The New Testament is set in the Roman Empire at a time when slavery was widespread and cruelty to slaves was at or near its peak. As explained in the book Slavery in the Roman Empire, masters sometimes killed their slaves or hacked their limbs off simply to entertain guests.

During this time, the apostle Paul sent to churches and individuals various letters that became a significant part of the New Testament. In these letters, Paul makes several references to slavery, such as one in the book of Ephesians, in which Paul tells slaves to be obedient to their masters.

At first glance, one might think this passage is supportive of slavery. However, the same passage also instructs masters not to threaten their slaves and to treat them "in the same way" slaves are to treat their masters. How could the institution of slavery exist under such guidelines? The answer is that it can't. So why doesn't Paul directly tell masters to set their slaves free?

This is where historical context becomes important. The Roman historian Suetonius recorded that in the era when Jesus was born, the emperor Augustus enacted "many obstacles to either the partial or complete emancipation of slaves." Thus, instead of calling for the release of slaves that would have resulted in a fruitless conflict with the Roman Empire, Paul undercut the institution of slavery by advancing values that are irreconcilable with it.

Some have tried to put a different slant on Paul's words by creatively interpreting them from the viewpoint that slavery was a benefit to the slaves, but we know Paul didn't think this way because in the first letter to Timothy, Paul included "slave traders" in a list of "ungodly and sinful" people. Furthermore, he wrote the following in his first letter to the Corinthians: "Were you a slave when you were called? Don't let it trouble you -- although if you can gain your freedom, do so."

Paul, in compliance with Roman law, sent a slave [Onesimus] back to his master but told the master to welcome this person as he would welcome Paul himself: "no longer as a slave," but as a "dear brother." Then he boldly enjoined the master to do "even more than I ask." These were obviously instructions to set Onesimus free, or at the very least treat him as such if there were legal impediments to actually freeing him.

Also note how Paul used the term "brother." This carries profound implications that ring throughout his writings, such as the letter to the Galatians, which states, "You are all sons of God through faith in Christ Jesus. ... There is neither Jew nor Greek, slave nor free, male nor female, for you are all one in Christ Jesus."

A minister named Charles Elliot eloquently articulated the same point in a book published two years before the start of the U.S. Civil War:

> To apply the terms brethren and sisters to slaves, initiates a new element into the subject unknown to all slave laws, and all slavery principles. In the West Indies the pro-slavery men ... ridiculed the idea of brothers and sisters among the missionary Churches. They asked, "Can you make your negroes Christians, and use the words dear brother or sister, to those you hold in bondage? They would conceive themselves, by possibility, put on a level with yourselves, and the chains of slavery would be broken."

He also provided a poignant summary of the New Testament's response to the Roman slave system:

> To have preached the emancipation of slaves, by the apostles, would have been the same as to attempt an overthrow of the Roman Government. And this civil emancipation would not strike at the root of the evil. Our Lord and his apostles, therefore, went to the source of the evil, by preaching the Gospel to both slaves and masters; so that, in carrying out the moral principles of our holy religion, and a moral practice under it, the great moral evils of the world were undermined.

...the Bible is a radically anti-slavery document, and this is proven not only by the words in it, but by the actions of the people who faithfully applied and still continue to apply the principles that it espouses.

–americanthinker.com/2012/05/what_dan_savage_doesnt_know_about_the_bible_and_slavery.html

—Other Notes—

ANSWERS

1. Expectation
2. Ephesus
3. False doctrine
4. Fables and endless genealogies
5. Purity of heart, a good conscience, and unfeigned faith
6. The Law
7. The knowledge of sin, a good life
8. No, he kept in mind his sin nature
9. The preaching he had received (prophecyings) and his faith.
10. Hymenaeus and Alexander
11. Supplication, Prayers, Intercession, Thanksgiving
12. To lead a quiet and peaceable life
13. For people to get saved
14. One
15. He gave Himself a ransom for all.
16. With holiness
17. Not in show
18. Men

The Qualification of Ministers – 1 Timothy 3:1-16
19. Bishop (overseer), Pastor, Elder, Deacon
20. blameless, husband of one wife, vigilant, sober, good behavior, hospitable, apt to teach, not given to wine, no striker, not greedy, patient, not a brwler, not covetous, one that rules his own house, have a good report
21. grave, not double tongued, not given to wine, not greedy of filthy lucre, pure conscience in mystery of faith, blameless, husband of one wife, ruling home
22. spiritual vs. physical work
23. To set the pattern for ministry in the church.
24. That God was manifest in the flesh
25. Hypocritical lying, Forbidding to marry, commanding to abstain from meats
26. Old wives' fables, Bodily exercise
27. Those who believe
28. Being an example in word, conversation (lifestyle), charity, spirit, faith purity; Reading the Bible, Exhorting (encouraging) each other, Doctrine

Ministry in the Church – 1 Timothy 5:1-6:2

29. Older men as fathers, younger men as brothers
30. Older women as mothers and younger women as sisters, widows should be cared for as a family member
31. Widows indeed and widows that live in pleasure
32. They should first be provided for by their family, and then by the church if they are doing all they can to serve God.
33. Double honor (pay)
34. Receive an accusation with two or three witnesses, rebuke the guilty publicly
35. Exercising partiality
36. Laying hands on people suddenly, joining in with others sins
37. Grape juice
38. Don't be so anxious to deal with every problem in the most extreme way possible.
39. Worthy of honor and respect, both participating in the benefits of the work

Encouragement to Ministers – 1 Timothy 6:3-21

40. He does not have wholesome words and good doctrine, He is proud, knowing nothing, argumentative, filled with envy, strife, railings, evil assumptions, perverse disputings, corrupt minds, destitute of truth, living for money
41. Godliness with contentment
42. Money
43. righeousness, godliness, love, patience, meekness, things of eternal value, a good reputation
44. not trust in riches, but trust in God
45. profane and vain babllings and opposition of false science

Thankfulness for the Soldier of Christ – 2 Timothy 1:1-7

46. praying for him day and night
47. unfeigned faith
48. Timothy's mother and grandmother
49. power,love, a sound mind

The Call of a Soldier of Christ – 2 Timothy 1:8-18

50. His Christian testimony, Paul, the afflictions of the Gospel
51. Because we know whom we have believed
52. The form of sound words that we have received through preaching

The Character of a Soldier of Christ – 2 Timothy 2:1-26

53. Be stong

54. commit the truths learned to faithful men

55. Entangling himself with the affairs of this life, striving unlawfully

56. The fruits of the ministry

57. We shall be victorious in the resurrection because Christ is faithful

58. The resurrection and the doctrines they had learned, avoiding clever speech designed to take advantage of people

59. Study to find approval from God

60. Increase ungodliness that eats as a cancer

61. By sanctification prepared for every good work

62. Avoid youthful lusts and foolish questions

63. Be anxious to help people learn and come to resolution

64. God

65. They will recover themselves out of the snare of the devil

The Caution of a Soldier of Christ – 2 Timothy 3:1-17

66. perilous times

67. Lovers of self, covetous, boasters, proud, blasphemers, disobedient to parents, unthankful, unholy, without natural affection, trucebreakers, false accusers, incontinent, fierce, despisers of those that are good, traitors, heady, highminded, lovers of pleasures more than lovers of God.

68. Resisting the truth, corrupt, reprobate concerning the faith

69. No

70. Doctrine, manner of life, purpose, faith, longsuffering, charity, patience, the kinds of persecution he got over doctrine

71. Persecution for godly living

72. No

73. Learning God's Word

74. By inspiration

75. Doctrine, Reproof, Correction, Instruction in Righteous

76. We will be thoroughly equipped to serve God

The Charge to a Soldier of Christ – 2 Timothy 4:1-5

77. God

78. Preach the Word

79. In season, out of season
80. Reprove, rebuke, exhort, do it with lonngsuffering and doctrine
81. Heap to themselves teachers, turn their ears from the truth, turn to fables
82. Watch in all things, endure afflictions, do the work of an evangelist

The Comfort of a Soldier of Christ – 2 Timothy 4:6-22

83. To be offered up to God and his departure from earth
84. He fought the good fight, he had finished his course, he kept the faith
85. The crown of righteousness from the righteous judge.
86. Demas had a love for the world, Mark had a love for the ministry (not just that Demas left Paul while Mark was profitable)
87. His cloke which he had loaned out, books and parchments.
88. Let God reward him according to his works, be aware of him
89. For God's deliverance
90. A desire for God's grace in Timothy's life

The Need for Mature Leadership – Titus 1:1-16

91. Before the world began
92. Through preaching
93. To ordain elders in every city
94. blameless, once married, faithful children who are not unruly, a steward of God, not self-willed, not soon angry, not give to wine, not a fist fighter, greedy of money, lover of hospitality and good men, sober, just, holy, temperate
95. Unruly and vain talkers and deceivers
96. Liars, beasts, slow bellies
97. rebuke them sharply, don't get caught up in conspiracy theories
98. Unto the pure all things are pure, unto the defiled and unbelieving is nothing pure, their conscience is defiled

The Character of Mature Believers in Leadership – Titus 2:1-15

99. Use sound doctrine
100.   sober, grave, temperate, sound in faith, charity, and patience
101.   maintain behavior that is becoming to holiness, not false accusers, not given to wine, teaching good things
102.   To be sober, love their husbands and children, be discreet, chaste, keepers at home, good, obedient to husbands

103. Sound speech

104. Be obedient to employers, not answering back, not stealing, showing good faith

105. Looking for that blessed hope, the resurrection at the appearing of Jesus Christ

106. Speak, exhort, and rebuke with all authority

General Charge for Mature Believers – Titus 3:1-15

107. Be subject to them

108. For we ourselves also were sometimes foolish, disobedient, and deceived

109. Good works are good and profitable unto men

110. After the first and second admonition

Received in the Bonds of Love – 1:1-25

111. He had a church in his house

112. love, faith, integrity (good things that made his communications effective), blessing for saints

113. He was converted while Paul was old and in bonds

114. A genuine conversion: he was now profitable for the ministry

115. He would not do it without the permission of Philemon

116. Even though Onesimus had run away, he ended up getting saved and was more than a servant now

117. He and Philemon were partners in ministry

118. He offered to pay any obligations Onesimus had to Philemon

119. Paul had been such a big blessing to Philemon

120. Be released and visit Philemon

121. The sinner who had been unprofitable to the Father was graciously made acceptable and became profitable to the ministry. Jesus paid any debts and because of the special loving relationship and partnership between Him and the Father it is to be expected that the Father will honor the Son's request. In the end all will be brought together in glory.

Made in United States
Orlando, FL
15 July 2024

48991153R00028